From the Library of
Mrs. Winters

# CHLOE KIM

## Gold Medal Star

# CHLOE KIM

Gold
Medal
Star

SUSAN TAYLOR

22 MediaWorks

Copyright © 2018 by 22MediaWorks

ISBN 978-1-338-32962-9

10 9 8 7 6 5 4 3 2 1    18 19 20 21 22

Printed in the U.S.A.      40
First printing 2018

Book produced by 22MediaWorks
Graphic design by Fabia Wargin

PHOTOS ©: Alamy, Associated Press,
Got it! / KPark Kühtai, iStock, Shutterstock

# You may have heard of Chloe Kim.

She is best known as one of the top snowboarders in the world today. At the 2018 Winter Olympics in PyeongChang, South Korea, she won gold in halfpipe with a jaw-dropping set of flips, twists, and altitude-seeking tricks. Aside from her status as an Olympic athlete, Chloe is a typical teenager. But her weekends look a bit different than those of your average high school senior.

**"I always get the question, like,**

**'Where are you from?'**

**L.A.**

**'No, where are you *really* from?'**

**I was born in Long Beach.**

**'No, no, like, where are yo really, *really* from?'"**

# The Making of a Champion

**Chloe gets a lot of motivation** from her parents, who emigrated from South Korea to California in the 1980s. "Watching my family work hard has been inspirational. I got their work ethic," Chloe says. Although she still has close connections to her extended family in South Korea, Chloe thinks of herself as a typical American teen, preferring KFC and In-N-Out to her mom's Korean dishes.

Chloe was born in California in 2000 and has spent most of her life in Southern California. "I'm so used to America, used to the traffic in L.A.," Chloe explains. "But obviously I have a Korean face, and I feel like that's just—you know, I can't walk around people like I'm straight-up American. I'm Korean-American. My parents are from Korea."

Thirteen-year-old Chloe Kim run during the snowboarding superpipe final at the Dew Tour iON Mountain Championships, December 14, 2013, in Breckenridge, Colorado.

France

Los Angeles,
California

Switzerland

**These days, more than anything else, Chloe** sees herself as a competitive snowboarder. She started early—tightening her first bindings at age 4. Her dad, Jong Kim, introduced her to the sport because he wanted a partner with whom to learn snowboarding. But Chloe quickly outpaced her dad. "When I learned how to turn, he was still struggling how to get off the chairlift," she says fondly.

Still, it wasn't love at first sight. "I wasn't so sure about the sport when I first started, but as I went snowboarding more and started progressing, I started to fall in love with it. I just think I had more fun snowboarding when I was able to go into the air and do spins and flips."

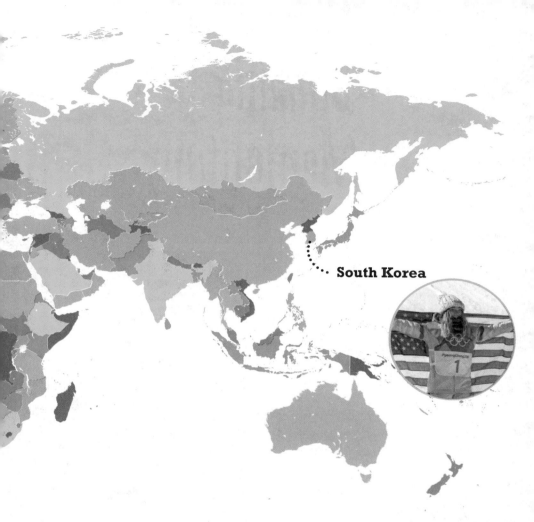

**South Korea**

Before kindergarten, Chloe was already hitting jumps and rails on weekends. At 6 years old, she joined a competitive team at Mountain High Resort near Los Angeles. Just one year later, she won Junior Nationals. Her star was rising. Fast.

When she was 8, Chloe moved to Switzerland so she could learn French. She lived with her aunt but couldn't stay away from snowboarding. Every weekend she would wake up at 4 a.m. and take two trains to a nearby resort across the border in France, where she could practice on a halfpipe. If that seems crazy—it was! Even Chloe admits that her childhood was far from average. But her path was clear. At an early age, she was determined to conquer the halfpipe before she got her driver's license.

# Building Momentum

**When Chloe moved back to** California two years later, her dad quit his job to help her train on more challenging terrain. Every weekend, Chloe and her dad drove five and a half hours to Mammoth Mountain near Mammoth Lakes, California, so she could train with top coaches. Her parents were motivated to see her win.

In 2014, Chloe showed what she was made of at ESPN's X Games. Coming in second behind 30-year-old superstar Kelly Clark, Chloe won silver and made history as the youngest person to earn a medal at the X Games. She was in eighth grade and only 13 years old.

Women's halfpipe would never be the same. Chloe took home gold at the X Games the next two years in a row, becoming the only athlete in X Games history to win three medals before the age of 16. She would have qualified for the 2014 Olympic Games in Sochi, Russia, but she missed the age cutoff. Instead, she spent her teenage years breaking other records.

# ALL ABOUT THE X GAMES

ESPN has hosted this annual sporting event since 1995. From skate-boarding and snowmobile to motocross and snowboarding, extreme athletes compete for medals and prize money under the spotlight of TV and thousands of spectators. The Winter X Games are held in Aspen, Colorado.

# Timeline

- First place in halfpipe at the X Games in Aspen, CO

- First place in halfpipe at the X Games in Aspen, CO

- Second place in halfpipe at the X Games in Aspen, CO

- First place in halfpipe at the U.S. Grand Prix in Park City, UT, where she earned a perfect score

- First place in halfpipe and slopestyle at the Winter Youth Olympic Games in Norway

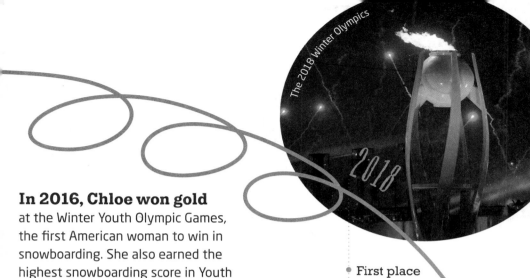

The 2018 Winter Olympics

**In 2016, Chloe won gold**
at the Winter Youth Olympic Games, the first American woman to win in snowboarding. She also earned the highest snowboarding score in Youth Olympic Games history and served as the U.S. flag bearer, the first snowboarder to do so.

At 16 years old, Chloe was making her mark in the snowboarding world. While she patiently waited for her chance to compete at the 2018 Winter Olympics, she gathered other accolades, such as an ESPY (ESPN's athlete award) and a position on *Time* magazine's list of the 30 most influential teens.

• First place in halfpipe at the Olympics in PyeongChang, South Korea

Chloe arrives at the 2016 ESPY Awards.

**Off the mountain, Chloe is a bubbly** and enthusiastic teenager. Her blonde highlights (and sometimes red, purple, or blue) could belong to any other high school senior. She uses social media often. She plays the guitar, loves animals, and practices turns on her skateboard when the snow melts. On the surface, she's a typical American teen. Except that she's also one of the top snowboarders in the world.

Just like many other teens, she's still figuring out who she is. "I'm, like, finishing up high school. I don't know how you can learn anything from me because I'm still a teenager," she said in an interview. "I don't know what I'm doing with my life." But she continues to inspire others, with more than 750,000 followers on Instagram and more than 300,000 on Twitter.

## FOLLOW CHLOE!

**INSTAGRAM:** @chloekimsnow

**TWITTER:** @chloekimsnow

**FACEBOOK:** @chloekimsnowboard

**SNAPCHAT:** chloekimsnow

# Top Tricks

**Chloe competes in two events:** slopestyle and halfpipe. In the sport of slopestyle, athletes do tricks on a terrain park. Halfpipe is a large ditch where snowboarders slide from one side to the other and perform tricks high in the air. In the Olympics, the halfpipe walls are 22 feet tall and snowboarders fly high above them. Talk about risky! While Chloe has competed in slopestyle (and won quite a few times), she focuses on halfpipe. Somehow, she doesn't let the risk get into her head.

A view of the SlopeStyle course at KPark, a freestyle snow park in Kühtai, Austria.

# HISTORY OF SNOWBOARDING

Snowboarding is related to other board sports, like surfing and skateboarding. Beginning in the 1960s, athletes adapted boards to use on snow. But not everyone immediately accepted the new winter sport. In the late 1970s, skiers tried to outlaw the new sport from traditional ski resorts. Luckily, skiers and snowboarders have since learned to live in harmony.

The first world championships of snowboarding were held in 1983. But the sport didn't officially join the Olympic lineup until the 1998 Games in Nagano, Japan. Two years later, Chloe Kim was born.

Fifteen-year-old Daniel Kandlbauer performs a jump with his snowboard on November 21, 1998, in Grindelwald, Switzerland, with the infamous Eiger north face as a backdrop.

**Chloe's signature trick is back-to-back 1080 spins.**
This means Chloe does three full revolutions in the air, in two successive turns through the halfpipe. She was the first woman to land this difficult combination. During a competition at the 2016 Grand Prix, her back-to-back 1080 spins helped her secure a perfect score of 100 points. Only one other snowboarder, Shaun White, has managed to achieve a perfect score.

If any of these daredevil tricks make her nervous, she doesn't show it. "I don't feel that much fear," she says. But just in case, Chloe leans down and knocks on her snowboard before every run. "You know how when you jinx yourself, they're, like, 'Knock on wood'? My snowboard's wood, so in case I jinxed myself sometime in the past, I knock on my board. It just makes me feel a lot more comfortable."

# The Competition

**Chloe is often the youngest competitor, but she isn't fazed** by older and more experienced snowboarders. "I don't get intimidated by competing against people older than myself, only because everyone's usually friends with their competitors in this industry, and it's a pretty laid-back vibe."

Chloe has identified two of her childhood heroes—Kelly Clark and Torah Bright—as her biggest inspirations. She has watched them win Olympic gold medals and push the boundaries in women's snowboarding. Since her debut in 2013, she has beaten both Kelly and Torah in competitions.

From left to right, Torah Bright (Silver) celebrates with Kaitlyn Farrington (Gold) and Kelly Clark (Bronze) at the flower ceremony for the women's halfpipe at the Sochi 2014 Winter Olympic Games.

## HERO SPOTLIGHT: TORAH BRIGHT

Australian snowboarder Torah Bright has paved the way for athletes like Chloe. In the 2010 Vancouver Olympics, despite two concussions during training and a crash during her first run, she won gold in halfpipe. She later earned silver in the 2014 Sochi Olympics. Unfortunately, Torah didn't make it to PyeongChang for the 2018 Olympics. A number of injuries kept her off the Australian snowboard team.

## > COMPETING AGAINST FRIENDS <

Kelly Clark, a 34-year-old who competed in four prior Olympics, trains at Mammoth Mountain alongside Chloe. Before PyeongChang, Kelly had already earned an Olympic gold medal and two bronze medals. She has also won seven X Games gold medals and 14 overall, making her the most decorated woman in X Games history. She was the first woman to land a 1080 in competition and is one of the most dominant snowboarders in history. During the 2017 PyeongChang test event, Kelly came in first, while Chloe came in fourth. Beating Kelly in the Olympics wouldn't be easy.

Chloe first met Kelly in a lift line at Mammoth Mountain. Chloe was only 8 years old when she asked to ride the lift alongside her hero. At left, five years later, at the 2014 X Games.

## As the 2018 Olympics loomed, Chloe stayed focused.

She needed to outperform some of the best snowboarders in the world. Two of her top competitors (and members of Team USA) were Kelly Clark and Arielle Gold. Although they are all friends, only one of them could take home gold.

From Steamboat Springs, Colorado, 21-year-old Arielle Gold was hoping to redeem herself after the 2014 Olympic Games in Sochi. During that contest, Arielle dislocated her shoulder just moments before her race, forcing her to sit on the sidelines. Over the next four years, Arielle set her sights on PyeongChang and a second chance in the Olympic spotlight.

ARIELLE GOLD

# Taking Home Gold

Above: A view of the halfpipe in the freestyle ski park, and the back of the viewing stand at the 2018 Winter Olympics.

Right: Chloe with figure skater Ashley Wagner at an event leading up to the Olympics.

**Expectations were high when Chloe arrived in** PyeongChang for the 2018 Winter Olympics. As soon as her plane landed in South Korea, she was followed closely by both American and Korean media. "It was actually really crazy; I had, like, a paparazzi moment there," Chloe told reporters, "which was kind of cool. I felt like Kim Kardashian . . . I look up, and there's like 25 cameras around."

Above left: Mascot of the 2018 Winter Games, Soohorang, the white tiger, and Bandabi, the Asiatic black bear mascot of the Paralympic Winter Games.

Throughout the opening ceremonies, and as the day of her race drew closer, Chloe mentally prepared herself to perform in front of thousands of spectators, as well as millions of TV viewers around the world. Despite the pressure, she pulled out a strong qualifying run and received the luxury of performing last during the finals on February 13. Eleven other snowboarders, including three other Americans, would battle her for the top spot.

## The week before

the race, athletes fought strong winds and dangerous weather conditions during their events, including the slopestyle competition one day earlier. But on the morning of the halfpipe event, the weather was perfect. Chloe woke up to sunny skies and light wind. Her family, including her 75-year-old grandmother from South Korea who had never seen Chloe compete, gathered in the stands to watch her race.

Chloe kept her cool, sending out a tweet: "Let's do this thing!"

On her first run, Chloe leaped into first place. She scored a 93.75, more than eight points higher than China's Jiayu Liu, who was knocked down to the second-place position. During round two, Chloe tried to land her signature back-to-back 1080 spins, but slipped and fell. Still, she held on to the lead.

### FUEL FOR A CHAMPION?

Chloe's favorite foods include Hawaiian pizza and Oreos.

During the Olympics, she tweeted about eating a breakfast sandwich, churros, and ice cream. After her win, she wanted to celebrate with a burger and fries. She is a growing teenager, after all.

25

**Each rider gave it her all during the third round,**
with fellow Americans Arielle Gold and Kelly Clark landing in the third and fourth spot, respectively. As each rider failed to beat Chloe's score, it became clear that she would remain in first place. Because she was the last snowboarder to compete in round 3, she could choose to safely saunter down the halfpipe and claim her victory at the bottom, or she could show off her skills one last time.

"Going to my third run I knew I had the gold," Chloe said. "But I also knew I wouldn't be satisfied taking the gold and knowing that I hadn't put down my best." So Chloe went big—throwing down back-to-back 1080s and earning a nearly perfect score of 98.25.

Chloe dedicated her win to her grandma. "This one's for Grams," Kim told the crowd after she won. She added, "I can't wait to go shopping with her."

First-place winner Chloe Kim, second-place winner Jiayu Liu, and third-place winner Arielle Gold.

# FANTASTICAL

## WHAT'S IN CHLOE'S EARBUDS?

Chloe listened to "Paparazzi" by Lady Gaga during her first run and "MotorSport" by Migos, Cardi B, and Nicki Minaj for her third run.

**In the end, Chloe's patience and determination paid off.**
"When I couldn't make the team in Sochi due to my age—it felt like such a long journey. You know, going from 13 to 17 is such a big time gap. But at the end of the day, I'm here—and I'm happy." As the youngest woman to win an Olympic snowboarding medal, Chloe has a bright future ahead.

Bronze medalist Arielle Gold (USA), gold medalist Chloe Kim (USA), silver medalist Jiayu Liu (China) at the medal ceremony of ladies' halfpipe finals of snowboard at the 2018 PyeongChang Winter Olympic Games on February 13, 2018.

**Friend and competitor Arielle Gold isn't fooled by Chloe's young age. "Chloe is mature beyond her years. I'm grateful to share the podium with her."**

After the Olympics, Chloe returned home and enjoyed immediate fame. She landed on the cover of *Sports Illustrated* magazine. She appeared on Jimmy Fallon and other late-night talk shows. And she continues to work with sponsors such as Burton Snowboards, Toyota, and Nike. Meanwhile, she's preparing for her high school graduation, planning for prom, and deciding which college to attend.

Chloe throws the first pitch before a MLB game between the San Francisco Giants and the Los Angeles Dodgers on April 1, 2018, at Dodger Stadium in Los Angeles, CA.

**For the next few years,** Chloe will train for the 2022 Olympics in Beijing. Up-and-comers such as Kelly Sildaru, who broke Chloe's record as the youngest gold medalist at the X Games, and experienced pros like Arielle Gold will be looking to overtake Chloe as the halfpipe champion. And while Chloe enjoys the competition, she insists that the most important thing for her is that the sport continues to be fun.

"I don't snowboard to win everything. I do it because I love it. I do it because I have fun, and everyone else can think whatever they want. For me, it's all about fun and I enjoy it so much."

For her thousands of fans, watching her break records, land back-to-back 1080s, and collect gold medals may be just as much fun.

Chloe Kim, first, and Haruna Matsumoto, third, celebrate after the Women's Halfpipe Final for the Burton U.S. Open Snowboarding Championships, March 10, 2018.

# CHLOE KIM